Art in the Street

Contents	Page
Cities and towns	2-3
Statues	4-5
Modern sculptures	6-7
Murals	8-9
Chalk art	10-11
Yarn art	12-13
Portrait Artists	14-15
Street performances	16-17
Buskers	18-19
Mime Artists	20-21
Art in the street	22-23
Index	24

written by Rosalind Hayhoe

Where is art?

Cities and towns are made up of lots of roads and buildings and houses. To help make them more interesting and beautiful places to live in or to visit, there are different kinds of art outside in the streets or in the parks. Art can be serious, or sometimes just for fun. Art can be permanent like a statue, or it might only be there for a short time like a chalk drawing.

Statues

In most cities there are statues of famous people, animals, or important events in history. They are often placed outside an important building in the town or in a park. Statues are usually carved out of stone or made with bronze. A notice underneath the statue tells people about the person or animal and why they were important. Some statues are very old – maybe even hundreds of years old.

Modern sculptures

Sculptures are large pieces of art that are made out of stone, wood, metal or plastic. Modern sculptures can be very unusual designs and sometimes they have moving parts. They don't always look like a person or an object, but they have a shape that represents or shows the artist's idea. You need to use your imagination to understand what they are supposed to be!

Murals on walls

To brighten up a dull area, sometimes an artist is asked to paint a large picture called a mural on the wall of a building. The mural might show people or animals, or it could be an interesting design with different patterns. The artist paints a clear coat of paint on the finished mural to protect it from the sun and rain. Murals help to make people feel better about living in an area where there might not be many trees or parks.

Art with chalk

Chalk Artists create amazing pictures on a flat area of paving (like a square) with big pieces of artists' chalk and powder. People like to stop and watch the artist drawing. Some of the art work is 3D and plays tricks on people by making the picture look deeper than it is. A Chalk Artist can spend up to four days drawing a picture, but it will fade away in the sun, or be washed away by the next rain.

11

Art surprises

Another type of street art that doesn't last for a long time is Yarn Art. This is when wool or string is knitted or crocheted around things in public places. An old statue may suddenly be wearing some knitted clothes, or trees in the park might have striped knitting around their trunks! This kind of street art surprises people and makes them smile.

Pictures to sell

On a busy street you can see artists painting pictures to sell. People can buy a painting from the artist and take it home. Some Artists paint pictures of a famous building or park. Portrait Artists paint pictures of people. They might paint a lifelike picture of the person, but sometimes they paint a funny cartoon picture of the person, called a caricature.

Street shows

Performance Artists are people who entertain us by performing a show in the street. It may be a group of actors or dancers who perform to an audience, or a clown or juggler who makes people laugh. Acrobats or fire-eaters are also Performance Artists. Some cities have a festival where many different types of street performers come to perform for people over a few days.

Busking for money

One of the most common types of street performance is busking: when a person sings or plays music on the street to earn some money. If people like their performance, they can put some money in the busker's instrument case or hat to show their appreciation. A good busker can gather a large crowd and make a lot of money. Some very well-known singers and musicians started out busking on the streets before they became famous.

Living statues

Some buskers are very loud, but others are very quiet! Mime Artists do not speak at all. They act out a story using only their body, eyes and mouth to show whether they are happy, sad or surprised. Some Mime Artists pretend to be a living statue. They paint their face and body to look like a statue and stand very still for a long time. People walking past don't know that the performer is a real person until the 'statue' suddenly moves!

Enjoy art!

Enjoy all the art that is in the parks or on the streets. Look at a sculpture and try to understand what the artist wants to show us, or learn the history of your town by finding out about the statues.

Stop and listen to a busker singing or watch a juggler perform. Look around and see how many different types of art you can see in your town.

Index	**Page**
Artists	6, 8, 10, 14, 16, 20, 22
busker	18, 20, 23
chalk	2, 10
design	6, 8
famous	4, 14, 18
history	4, 22
paint	8, 14, 20
parks	2, 4, 8, 12, 14, 22
performance	16, 18, 20, 23
stone	4, 6